BEHOLD THE HUMMINGBIRD!

To Jim and Ann, hummingbird helpers extraordinaire
—S. S.

To Noni and Nina, with much love and appreciation
for being part of my life
—T. G.

Published by
PEACHTREE PUBLISHING COMPANY INC.
1700 Chattahoochee Avenue
Atlanta, Georgia 30318-2112
PeachtreeBooks.com

Text © 2024 by Suzanne Slade
Illustrations © 2024 by Thomas Gonzalez

Edited by Kathy Landwehr
Design and composition by Lily Steele

Illustrations created in pastel, colored pencils, and airbrush.

Printed and bound in December 2023 at Toppan Leefung, DongGuan, China.
10 9 8 7 6 5 4 3 2 1
First Edition
ISBN: 978-1-68263-652-7

Cataloging-in-Publication Data is available from the Library of Congress.

Photo credits
page 28: Broad-billed Hummingbird (Stephen McPike ©2023); Blue-throated Hillstar Hummingbird (Jorge F. Humbser, The Art of Feathers ©2023)

page 29: Costa's Hummingbird (Gail West ©2013); Broad-billed Hummingbird (Gail West ©2011)

BEHOLD THE HUMMINGBIRD!

Written by **SUZANNE SLADE**

Illustrated by **THOMAS GONZALEZ**

PEACHTREE
ATLANTA

Amazing hummingbird!

Two tiny wings,

swift and strong,

soar through sapphire skies . . .

The hummingbird may be small, but it's also powerful and quick. These tiny flyers aren't easy to find, so people are excited when they spot one! Scientists have discovered at least 353 different types of hummingbirds, each with its own unique colors and design. The Ruby-throated Hummingbird (*Archilochus colubris*) is the only species that lives on the East Coast of the United States.

humming,

The hummingbird gets its name from the gentle humming sound created by its rapidly beating wings. This swift wing speed results in remarkable flying feats! It is the only bird that can fly backward and hover in one place like a helicopter. It can also maneuver up and down like an elevator or soar upside down while doing midair flips! To uncover the wing speed of these aerial acrobats, scientists use high-speed photography. The wings of a flap-happy Amethyst Woodstar (*Calliphlox amethystina*) hum along at 80 beats per second.

feeding,

A big eater, the hummingbird consumes half of its body weight in food every day! Sweet nectar from flowers provides sugar for energy. A hummingbird uses its long, thin bill to reach inside a bloom, then draws in nectar with its tongue. It may also drink sugar water from bird feeders, which offers bird-watchers a close-up peek! The impressive bill of the Sword-billed Hummingbird (*Ensifera ensifera*) can grow up to 4.7 inches (12 centimeters) long—which in some cases is as long as its body! It feeds on flowers with long corollas, or tubes, such as the bright pink *Passiflora mixta* blooms. To supply its busy body with protein and fat, it also dines on insects.

resting,

Searching for food requires a lot of energy, so a hummingbird often rests on a branch between meals. During that break it may also groom, or clean, its feathers. At night, a hummingbird looks for a twig in a leafy area where it can sleep, protected from the wind. When the weather turns cold, most species, including the Anna's Hummingbird (*Calypte anna*), go into a deep sleep called torpor. During torpor, a bird's breathing and heart rate slow and its temperature drops, which allows its tiny body to conserve energy. Torpor lasts from eight to fourteen hours, during which time the bird gets a nice long rest.

calling,

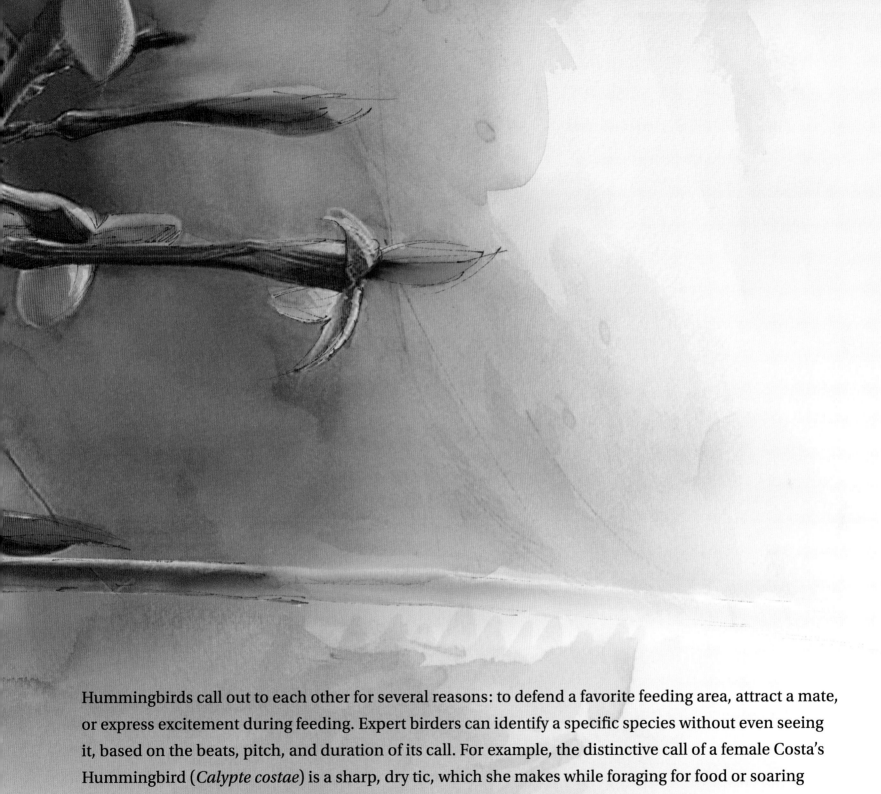

Hummingbirds call out to each other for several reasons: to defend a favorite feeding area, attract a mate, or express excitement during feeding. Expert birders can identify a specific species without even seeing it, based on the beats, pitch, and duration of its call. For example, the distinctive call of a female Costa's Hummingbird (*Calypte costae*) is a sharp, dry tic, which she makes while foraging for food or soaring through the air. The male rarely calls out. He prefers to sing his favorite song—four short, thin notes—while perched on a branch.

courting,

A hummingbird lives alone most of its life. But during courting, it finds a temporary mate. Some males perform mating dives with soaring loops and zigzags to get the attention of a female. The male Marvelous Spatuletail (*Loddigesia mirabilis*) has a special weapon to attract a lady—his long tail. At the communal area where females gather to find a mate, he puts on a spectacular display by hovering in front of a female. Then he waves the two spatula-shaped feathers at the end of his long, wirelike tail. If she likes the show, she may agree to be his mate (for a little while at least!). And with any luck, this courtship will result in an egg or two, because the Marvelous Spatuletail is currently endangered.

nesting.

When it's time to build a nest to hatch eggs and raise babies, the female hummingbird is on her own. A Rufous Hummingbird (*Selasphorus rufus*) female builds her nest in a leafy bush or a tree such as a spruce, pine, birch, or maple. The secret to creating her soft, sturdy home is spiderwebs. She uses the sticky material to hold grass, moss, and other plant materials together. She may add more moss, lichens, and bark on the outside of the nest to camouflage it from enemies. The inside of her completed nest is just 1 inch (2.5 centimeters) in diameter. Hummingbird nests may be reused the next year, though not always by the same mother.

Industrious,

As a hummingbird dines on hundreds of flowers each day, it performs another critical job—pollination. Tiny pollen grains from the flowers stick to its feathers and bill when it sips nectar from blooms. When that bird visits other flowers, bits of pollen fall off and pollinate them, creating new seeds. The Red-tailed Comet (*Sappho sparganurus*) pollinates colorful trees, herbs, and bushes in South American mountains. In fact, several plants depend on this species for pollination because the shape of their flowers doesn't allow pollinators like bees or butterflies to access them. A Red-tailed Comet may hang on certain flowers while feeding, which makes transferring pollen even easier.

ferocious,

When it comes to food, the hummingbird doesn't like to share. It will guard its feeding territory by launching a midair attack on intruders. The Sparkling Violetear (*Colibri coruscans*) is one of the most aggressive hummingbirds. It fiercely protects flowers containing nectar with the highest sugar content (often red, tubular-shaped blooms). To defend these precious blooms against unwelcome birds, moths, or bees, it may use a special scare tactic—flaring the blue-violet feathers on its head.

ambitious,

The Calliope Hummingbird (*Selasphorus calliope*) is the smallest hummingbird in North America. Though it's only 3 inches (7.6 centimeters) long, beak to tail, this tiny bird is an incredible flyer. Each year it migrates about 5,000 miles (8,000 kilometers) from western US states like California or Nevada to southern Mexico, where it enjoys warm weather during the winter. Unlike some migrating birds, the Calliope Hummingbird doesn't travel in groups. It embarks on its long migration all alone. Males usually begin their journeys first, and the females take off later.

and simply stupendous!

A hummingbird is covered with hundreds of shiny feathers. But this is no ordinary plumage! A hummer's iridescent feathers shimmer like jewels. Scientists say the unique iridescence is created by layers of teeny, tiny air bubbles within the feathers that reflect and refract sunlight. Similar to other birds, a male hummingbird's feathers are usually more colorful than those of a female of the same species. One particularly vibrant bird is the Fiery-throated Hummingbird (*Panterpe insignis*). This rainbow-colored stunner makes its home in the cloud forests (tropical forests with low-level clouds) of Costa Rica and Panama.

Behold,

the magnificent hummingbird

brightens the world with its beauty.

To ensure that beauty never ends,

a doting mother carefully tends

to her precious babies.

And before long,

fledglings venture from the nest

to begin their new lives

in the clear blue skies.

The world's smallest bird, the Bee Hummingbird (*Mellisuga helenae*), is only found in Cuba. Measuring 2.25 inches (5.75 centimeters) long, and weighing less than 0.07 ounces (2 grams), the weight of a dime, it is often mistaken for a large bee. The mother lays one or two oval, pea-sized eggs in her tiny nest. She keeps them warm by diligently sitting on them for two to three weeks. When the itty-bitty, blind babies with no feathers emerge from their shells, she hunts for food for herself and then feeds them her regurgitated meals. About three weeks after hatching, the brave fledglings leave their cozy nest to set off on their own.

FINDING HUMMINGBIRDS

Spotting a hummingbird is an unexpected, magical experience. But where can you find these busy beauties? Hummingbirds only live in the Americas (North, Central, and South America). This means people in Asia, Africa, Australia, and Europe won't see a hummer unless they travel far from home.

More than half of all known hummingbird species are found in the Andes Mountains, the longest mountain range in the world. This vast area spans Venezuela, Colombia, Ecuador, Peru, Bolivia, Argentina, and Chile.

Only fourteen species breed regularly in the United States and about five other varieties visit sometimes. Sunny Arizona attracts more hummingbird species

This gorgeous Blue-throated Hillstar Hummingbird (*Oreotrochilus cyanolaemus*) was photographed in Loja, Ecuador.

than any other state. Some live in Arizona year-round, while others stop there to rest as they migrate south to avoid the cold winter months. In Canada, five hummingbird species are commonly seen flitting about, while a few others pop in occasionally.

Fortunately, new types of hummingbirds are still being discovered. In 2017, ornithologist Francisco Sornoza spotted a hummer with an emerald-green and blue head during a hike in the Andes Mountains. He'd never seen a species with that head coloring before, so he took photos and shared them with colleagues. In time, they realized he'd stumbled upon a new hummingbird species, which was named the Blue-throated Hillstar (*Oreotrochilus cyanolaemus*). It's exciting to think of the brilliant hummingbirds yet to be uncovered.

The Broad-billed Hummingbird (*Cynanthus latirostris*) usually makes its home in Mexico, but it may visit Arizona and other southwestern states during the breeding season.

HELPING HUMMERS

Hummingbirds need to eat a lot of food every day to survive, so they're constantly searching for insects and nectar-filled flowers. If you live in an area with hummingbirds, you can help.

A Costa's Hummingbird (*Calypte costae*) dines on a purple flower called salvia.

Hummingbirds find flowers by sight, not smell. To attract them to your yard, plant red, orange, or dark pink tubular, native flowering plants. Hummers particularly like bee balm, butterfly bush, California fuchsia, cleome, columbine, coral bells, daylily, foxglove, hollyhock, honeysuckle, impatiens, lantana, lupine, mimosa, petunia, and trumpet creeper. Many of these plants are only found in certain climates, so you should research which grow in your area. Amazingly, a hummingbird remembers which specific blooms it's dined on, and won't visit them again until enough time has passed for the flower to refill with nectar.

You might also put out a feeder filled with sugar water. Because hungry hummingbirds are drawn to certain colored flowers, the color of the feeder is important. A red feeder works best; a yellow one will attract bees instead of birds. (But do not dye the water if you make your own sugar mixture. Dye can be harmful to hummingbirds.) Place the feeder near blooming flowers to help hummingbirds find it. Then step inside and watch for the amazing hummingbirds that stop by to visit!

A Broad-billed Hummingbird (*Cynanthus latirostris*) eats from a feeder filled with clear sugar water.

ACKNOWLEDGMENTS

My sincere appreciation to Dr. Jessie Williamson, Postdoctoral Fellow in the Department of Ecology & Evolutionary Biology and at the Lab of Ornithology, Cornell University, for reviewing the book's text and images. Special thanks to the Macaulay Library at the Cornell Lab of Ornithology for their assistance with photo research.

SELECTED BIBLIOGRAPHY

ABC's Bird Library, American Bird Conservancy. *abcbirds.org/birds*

Animal Diversity Web, University of Michigan Museum of Zoology. *animaldiversity.org*

eBird, The Cornell Lab of Ornithology, Cornell University. *ebird.org/home*

Eliason, Chad M., Rafael Maia, Juan L. Parra, and Matthew D. Shawkey, "Signal Evolution and Morphological Complexity in Hummingbirds (Aves: *Trochilidae*)." *Evolution*, Volume 74, Issue 2, 1 February 2020, pages 447–458. *doi.org/10.1111/evo.13893*

Guide to North American Birds, National Audubon Society. *audubon.org/bird-guide*

"Hummingbirds," Smithsonian's National Zoo & Conservation Biology Institute. *nationalzoo.si.edu/migratory-birds/hummingbirds*

"Hummingbirds at Chamizal," National Park Service, U.S. Department of the Interior. *www.nps.gov/cham/learn/nature/hummingbirds.htm*

LEARN MORE

All About Birds, The Cornell Lab of Ornithology, Cornell University. *allaboutbirds.org*

"Baby Hummingbirds: All You Need to Know (with Pictures)," Birdfact. *birdfact.com/articles/baby-hummingbirds*

"Interesting Facts on Hummingbirds," UC Davis Veterinary Medicine Hummingbird Health and Conservation Program. *hummingbirds.vetmed.ucdavis.edu/information/facts*

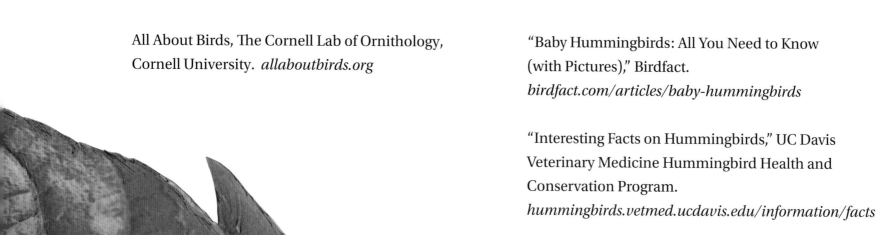